Anger Management for Inmates

KEITH ROYS

First Edition

ISBN-13: 978-1530865260

ISBN-10: 1530865263

Cover photo by Keith Roys

DEDICATION

This book is dedicated to all inmates who want to learn more about God and His word and how to use it to help manage their anger. Make your growth a priority!

Table of Contents

Acknowledgements

Thanks to all those who have prayed, laughed, smiled, shared pizza, and have been an encouragement in the writing and reviewing of this book!

Thanks go out to: Keturah, John, Michelle, Jeff, Johnna, Shawn, Mandy, Aaron, Erin, Chris, Vicki, Scott, Bill, Mike, Jeffrey, Sarah, and Brian.

Specific thanks also to my amazing parents who continue to love me, believe in me, and encourage me all the time. Thank you Mom and Dad! I love you!

Salvation

You may not fully realize it yet, but God loves you enough to provide you a way to find Him and gain His peace in your troubled life! He wants you to come to him, confess your sins, and accept His free gift of salvation and forgiveness! If you are not 100% certain of your salvation, read the following verses and pray a prayer like the one on the next page.

Ephesians 2:8-9 says that it is only by God's grace that you can be saved. There is nothing that you can do to earn it or work for it.

Romans 3:23 says all have sinned....that means you too! Sin has been in every person's life since Adam and Eve. Sin means we cannot be in God's holy presence.

Romans 6:23 says the penalty for sin is death...that means eternal separation from God and heaven.

Romans 5:8 says that even though we are condemned sinners, God loves us so much that He sent His son to pay our death penalty.

Romans 10:9 says that all you need to do is confess with your mouth that Jesus is Lord, that He died on the cross for your sins, and believe that God raised Him from death to life eternal.

Through what Jesus did on the cross, substituting His life for yours and dying on the cross in your place, His blood washes you clean of all of your sins and allows you once again to be in God's holy presence and guarantees you eternal life in heaven with Him!

If you believe this, pray something like this:
Lord God, I am a sinner. I believe you love me enough that what Jesus did on the cross paid my sin debt forever. Through His death and resurrection I now have life eternal in heaven and I thank You for that! Please forgive me of all of my sins and help me now to use my time to grow strong in Your word and share your love with others who need to hear it. Amen.

1 John 1:9 says that if we confess our sins, He will forgive and cleanse us! Accept that promise as truth and shed your burden of guilt and shame. Go forth with renewed confidence and build your foundation daily on His word!

Talk to your Chaplain to find out about worship service times and Bible study classes. See the end of the book for information on additional resources.

Anger Management Overview

All of us have experienced anger, whether we were on the receiving end or whether we ourselves were the angry person. Unmanaged anger can lead to poor decision making and serious consequences. The goal of this study is to help you understand the Bible's perspective on anger and give you some tools to help manage and diffuse your anger.

This is a four week long program and can be used by a single person or as a group study. When used as part of a group study, it is recommended the Chaplain or one of the senior Christian leadership team members facilitate each session.

This is "open book" meaning you can use your Bible as you go through the book. That is the intent, to get you familiar with finding useful information in your Bible! Once completed, this book will become a great resource for you to refer to. A completion certificate is available too (see information in the back of the book on how to request it).

So pray for the Holy Spirit to guide you and to open the Word to you, start reading, and enjoy!

Week 1 – Overview & Bible verses

Let's start by taking a short quiz to assess your current understanding of anger. You will take the same quiz at the end of the course and it will be interesting to see the changes in your answers! There are no right or wrong answers, just write down your honest thoughts!

Pre-quiz

What is anger?

What makes me angry?

What do I do when I get angry?

What are 3 good Bible verses to remember about anger?

Here is a decent definition of anger:

   - a strong feeling of being upset or annoyed because of something wrong or bad;

   - a strong feeling of annoyance, displeasure, unfairness, or hostility;

    -the feeling that makes someone want to hurt other people, to shout, to lose control, etc.

Words that are similar to anger include: rage, vexation, exasperation, displeasure, crossness, irritation, irritability, indignation, pique, annoyance, fury, wrath, ire, outrage, and ill temper.

Did you know that the Bible has dozens of verses related to anger? Some of them are listed below. Read through each one of them slowly and let God speak to you and write down your thoughts. There is space provided below each verse for you to write what it means to you. Then go back and circle three that you find most meaningful to you and memorize them!

Psalm 4:4

Be angry, and do not sin; ponder in your own hearts on your beds, and be silent.

To me, this means: _____

_____

_____

_____

_____

Psalm 37:8-9

Refrain from anger, and forsake wrath! Fret not yourself; it tends only to evil. For the evildoers shall be cut off, but those who wait for the Lord shall inherit the land.

To me, this means: _____

_____

_____

_____

_____

Proverbs 12:16
The vexation of a fool is known at once, but the prudent ignores an insult.

To me, this means: _____

_____

_____

_____

_____

Proverbs 14:17
A man of quick temper acts foolishly, and a man of evil devices is hated.

To me, this means: _____

_____

_____

_____

_____

Proverbs 14:29
Whoever is slow to anger has great understanding, but he who has a hasty temper exalts folly.

To me, this means: _____

_____

_____

_____

_____

Proverbs 15:1
A soft answer turns away wrath, but a harsh word stirs up anger.

To me, this means: _____

_____

_____

_____

_____

Proverbs 15:5

A fool despises his father's instruction, but whoever heeds reproof is prudent.

To me, this means: _____

_____

_____

_____

_____

Proverbs 15:18

A hot-tempered man stirs up strife, but he who is slow to anger quiets contention.

To me, this means: _____

_____

_____

_____

_____

Proverbs 16:32

Whoever is slow to anger is better than the mighty, and he who rules his spirit than he who takes a city.

To me, this means: _____

_____

_____

_____

_____

Proverbs 19:11

Good sense makes one slow to anger, and it is his glory to overlook an offense.

To me, this means: _____

_____

_____

_____

_____

Proverbs 22:24
Make no friendship with a man given to anger, nor go with a wrathful man.

To me, this means: _____

_____

_____

_____

_____

Proverbs 25:28
A man without self-control is like a city broken into and left without walls.

To me, this means: _____

_____

_____

_____

_____

Proverbs 29:11

A fool gives full vent to his spirit, but a wise man quietly holds it back.

To me, this means: _____

_____

_____

_____

_____

Proverbs 29:22

A man of wrath stirs up strife, and one given to anger causes much transgression.

To me, this means: _____

_____

_____

_____

_____

Ecclesiastes 3:1-8

For everything there is a season, and a time for every matter under heaven: a time to be born, and a time to die; a time to plant, and a time to pluck up what is planted; a time to kill, and a time to heal; a time to break down, and a time to build up; a time to weep, and a time to laugh; a time to mourn, and a time to dance; a time to cast away stones, and a time to gather stones together; a time to embrace, and a time to refrain from embracing; a time to seek, and a time to lose; a time to keep, and a time to cast away; a time to tear, and a time to sew; a time to keep silence, and a time to speak; a time to love, and a time to hate; a time for war, and a time for peace.

To me, this means: _____

_____

_____

_____

_____

Ecclesiastes 7:9

Be not quick in your spirit to become angry, for anger lodges in the bosom of fools.

To me, this means: _____

_____

_____

_____

Matthew 5:21-24

You have heard that it was said to those of old, 'You shall not murder; and whoever murders will be liable to judgment.' But I say to you that everyone who is angry with his brother will be liable to judgment; whoever insults his brother will be liable to the council; and whoever says, 'You fool!' will be liable to the hell of fire. So if you are offering your gift at the altar and there remember that your brother has something against you, leave your gift there before the altar and go. First be reconciled to your brother, and then come and offer your gift.

To me, this means: _____

_____

_____

_____

_____

Matthew 7:1-5

Judge not, that you be not judged. For with the judgment you pronounce you will be judged, and with the measure you use it will be measured to you. Why do you see the speck that is in your brother's eye, but do not notice the log that is in your own eye? Or how can you say to your brother, 'Let me take the speck out of your eye,' when there is the log in your own eye? You hypocrite, first take the log out of your own eye, and then you will see clearly to take the speck out of your brother's eye.

To me, this means: _____

_____

_____

_____

_____

Matthew 11:28-30

Come to me, all who labor and are heavy laden, and I will give you rest. Take my yoke upon you, and learn from me, for I am gentle and lowly in heart, and you will find rest for your souls. For my yoke is easy, and my burden is light.

To me, this means: _____

_____

_____

_____

_____

Luke 6:31

And as you wish that others would do to you, do so to them.

To me, this means: _____

_____

_____

_____

_____

Romans 12:21

Do not be overcome by evil, but overcome evil with good.

To me, this means: _____

_____

_____

_____

_____

Galatians 5:19-20

Now the works of the flesh are evident: sexual immorality, impurity, sensuality, idolatry, sorcery, enmity, strife, jealousy, fits of anger, rivalries, dissensions, divisions…

To me, this means: _____

_____

_____

_____

_____

Galatians 5:22-23
But the fruit of the Spirit is love, joy, peace, patience, kindness, goodness, faithfulness, gentleness, self-control; against such things there is no law.

To me, this means: _____

_____

_____

_____

_____

Ephesians 4:18
They are darkened in their understanding, alienated from the life of God because of the ignorance that is in them, due to their hardness of heart.

To me, this means: _____

_____

_____

_____

_____

Ephesians 4:26-27

Be angry and do not sin; do not let the sun go down on your anger, and give no opportunity to the devil.

To me, this means: _____

_____

_____

_____

_____

Ephesians 4:31

Let all bitterness and wrath and anger and clamor and slander be put away from you, along with all malice.

To me, this means: _____

_____

_____

_____

_____

Philippians 4:4-6

Rejoice in the Lord always; again I will say, Rejoice. Let your reasonableness be known to everyone. The Lord is at hand; do not be anxious about anything, but in everything by prayer and supplication with thanksgiving let your requests be made known to God.

To me, this means: _____

_____

_____

_____

_____

Colossians 3:8

But now you must put them all away: anger, wrath, malice, slander, and obscene talk from your mouth.

To me, this means: _____

_____

_____

_____

_____

Colossians 3:13

…bearing with one another and, if one has a complaint against another, forgiving each other; as the Lord has forgiven you, so you also must forgive.

To me, this means: _____

_____

_____

_____

_____

1 Timothy 2:1-2

First of all, then, I urge that supplications, prayers, intercessions, and thanksgivings be made for all people, for kings and all who are in high positions, that we may lead a peaceful and quiet life, godly and dignified in every way.

To me, this means: _____

_____

_____

_____

_____

James 1:2-5

Count it all joy, my brothers, when you meet trials of various kinds, for you know that the testing of your faith produces steadfastness. And let steadfastness have its full effect, that you may be perfect and complete, lacking in nothing. If any of you lacks wisdom, let him ask God, who gives generously to all without reproach, and it will be given him.

To me, this means: _____

_____

_____

_____

_____

James 1:19-20

Know this, my beloved brothers: let every person be quick to hear, slow to speak, slow to anger; for the anger of man does not produce the righteousness of God.

To me, this means: _____

_____

_____

_____

_____

James 4:1-2

What causes quarrels and what causes fights among you? Is it not this, that your passions are at war within you? You desire and do not have, so you murder. You covet and cannot obtain, so you fight and quarrel. You do not have, because you do not ask.

To me, this means: _____

_____

_____

_____

_____

James 4:11-12

Do not speak evil against one another, brothers. The one who speaks against a brother or judges his brother, speaks evil against the law and judges the law. But if you judge the law, you are not a doer of the law but a judge. There is only one lawgiver and judge, he who is able to save and to destroy. But who are you to judge your neighbor?

To me, this means: _____

_____

_____

_____

<u>1 Peter 2:23</u>
When he was reviled, he did not revile in return; when he suffered, he did not threaten, but continued entrusting himself to him who judges justly.

To me, this means: _____

_____

_____

_____

_____

Don't forget to go back and circle the three verses that you want to memorize!

Week 2 – Triggers

Anger is not necessarily a bad emotion. It is your reaction to it and your behavior while angry that can get you into trouble. Uncontrolled yelling, screaming, cursing, and hitting things or people are all behaviors that will most likely lead to unfavorable results. You cannot always manage your feelings, but you do have some control over your reaction to your feelings and your behavior. You want to learn how to properly control your behavior when you are angry.

All sorts of things can get people angry. They can be things that are internal or external. Some things are common to most people and some will be unique to you. By the end of this book, you should be to:

- identify what triggers you are angry,

- recognize situations where they may arise,

- recognize signs that you are getting angry, and

- manage your reactions to the triggers in a safe, mature, and biblical manner.

In this section, we want to look at what triggers your anger. Take a look at the list on the next page and check which ones you believe trigger your anger. There are some blank lines at the end to add additional triggers you are aware of.

I get angry when…

__ someone causes a shakedown.
__ someone causes a lockdown.
__ the CO's irritate or pick on me.
__ the CO's canceled rec for no good reason.
__ the lines for chow are long.
__ someone in a gang harasses me.
__ I can't go to the funeral of a family member.
__ I don't get mail during mail call.
__ my commissary order gets screwed up.
__ I don't have enough money to buy commissary.
__ I can't get on the phone to make a call.
__ someone steals stuff from my locker.
__ someone says I weigh too much.
__ my cellmate forgets something I said.
__ my cellmate complains or worries.
__ my cellmate is noisy when I am trying to sleep.
__ other inmates are disrespectful to me.
__ other inmates try to pick a fight with me.
__ the CO's don't believe me.
__ the CO's give me too much work to do.
__ someone says mean things to me.
__ someone takes advantage of me.
__ someone ignores me.
__ someone makes fun of me.
__ someone accuses me falsely.
__ I think God treated me unfairly.

__ I am unappreciated.

__ someone breaks a promise.

__ someone lies to me.

__ someone lies about me.

__ the TV breaks down.

__ I don't get a class I wanted.

__ I don't get a visit I expected.

__ my release date is delayed.

__ I don't get parole.

__ some of my laundry is missing.

__ my favorite sports team loses.

__ a politician does something wrong.

__ I don't like a sermon.

__ a pastor or church leader ignores me.

__ my significant other doesn't write me.

__ my friends outside don't seem to care about me.

__ Other _____

__ Other _____

__ Other _____

__ Other _____

__ Other _____

__ Other _____

Pick three triggers that you checked above and write down what the situation was and then write down your specific trigger (or triggers) in that situation. Be honest with yourself! Just describe the situation for now. We will get to your reaction in the next chapter.

<u>Angry Situation #1</u>

The situation: _____

_____

_____

_____

_____

_____

_____

_____

My trigger(s): _____

_____

_____

_____

Angry Situation #2

The situation: _____

_____

_____

_____

_____

_____

_____

_____

My trigger(s): _____

_____

_____

_____

Angry Situation #3

The situation: _____

_____

_____

_____

_____

_____

_____

_____

My trigger(s): _____

_____

_____

_____

Week 3 – Reactions

Be honest with yourself. Which of the following reactions have you ever had when you were angry?

__ Yell or raise my voice
__ Hit, or want to hit, something or someone
__ Threaten someone
__ Try to get back at or get even with someone
__ Clenched fists
__ Get irritated
__ Get upset or grumpy
__ Make sarcastic comments
__ Put other people down
__ Get impatient or frustrated
__ Withdraw or pout
__ Turn to alcohol or drugs
__ Feel bitter
__ Feel resentful
__ Feel sorry for myself
__ Think angry thoughts
__ Other: _____
__ Other: _____
__ Other: _____

Take a look at Galatians 5:22-25.

> *But the fruit of the Spirit is love, joy, peace, patience, kindness, goodness, faithfulness, gentleness, self-control; against such things there is no law. And those who belong to Christ Jesus have crucified the flesh with its passions and desires. If we live by the Spirit, let us also keep in step with the Spirit.*

The nine listed items are the fruit of the Spirit. All Christians have these in their life but some may be more developed than others. Fruit takes time and cultivation to grow! If these are active in your daily life, they will absolutely help you minimize and manage your anger. Let's examine each one and see how it relates to anger.

1. Love: The Greek word used in this verse for love is *agape*. Of the four types of love mentioned in the Bible (see Appendix 2 for definitions of all four), agape love is unconditional, selfless, and sacrificial. If this type of love is an intentional conscious part of your daily life, it will be very difficult for anger to gain a foothold!

2. Joy: This refers to something more than simple happiness in your life. Joy means that you are not letting circumstances rule your life and that you find gladness and God's purpose in both the good

and bad things that you encounter daily. It means you take pause and prayerfully examine situations and seek God's purpose in each. Such an approach will not let anger rule your life.

3. Peace: this is what you experience regardless of earthly circumstances. It means you are focused on His purposes and trust completely in Him throughout your daily walk. Philippians 4:6-7 says:

    Do not be anxious about anything, but in everything by prayer and supplication with thanksgiving let your requests be made known to God. And the peace of God, which surpasses all understanding, will guard your hearts and your minds in Christ Jesus.

4. Patience: you really do have the ability to be patient! You just need to exercise it and practice it more often so that it becomes second nature to you. The drama of the world around you will not affect you as much because you exercise patience. When something flares up, you do not let it trigger an immediate angry response. Instead, you pause, you think, you pray, and you keep a cool head and make better decisions. The more you do this, the more you WILL do this!

Just think about the patience Jesus showed when
He was being tempted by Satan in the wilderness.
Jesus stayed calm and He used Scripture to help
stay focused. You too can be patient, stay calm,
and remember some good verses (like those in
Chapter 1) to help you manage your anger.

5. Kindness: When you are kind, and you experience
   a situation or problem, you are looking for ways to
   help meet the needs of others and you are NOT
   looking for ways to be angry or mean to others.
   Kindness wells up from the love in your heart and
   from your love for the Lord.

6. Goodness: God is good and when you too are
   good, you are reflecting His goodness to others.
   When you respond to anger by being loving,
   peaceful, patient, kind, and good, you bring calm
   to the situation, allow for tensions to diffuse and
   for clear thinking to prevail. What a great way to
   witness to others!

7. Faithfulness: A person who is faithful has integrity.
   They are known to be stable and steady and not
   easily rattled or angered. By reading His word
   daily, going to church on a regular basis, by
   fellowshipping with other believers, your faith will
   grow stronger and stronger. You will be better

prepared to handle your anger triggers and not allow them to rule your life.

8. Gentleness: this does not mean weakness or passivity. It does not mean you are a doormat or allow people to take advantage of you. It means you allow the love, peace, and wisdom of God to flow through you and into the relationships you have and into the situations you encounter every day. It means you forgive others easily and that you also can handle angry situations with love and calmness.

9. Self-control: Paul, in Romans 7:15-20, provides an excellent description of the battle that goes on inside us daily between the desires of the flesh and the desires of the Spirit.

> *For I do not understand my own actions. For I do not do what I want, but I do the very thing I hate. Now if I do what I do not want, I agree with the law, that it is good. So now it is no longer I who do it, but sin that dwells within me. For I know that nothing good dwells in me, that is, in my flesh. For I have the desire to do what is right, but not the ability to carry it out. For I do not do the good I want, but the evil I do not want is what I keep on doing. Now if I do what I do not want, it is no longer I who do it, but sin that dwells within me.*

This is the struggle that you cannot win in your own strength. It takes the power of God, through the Holy Spirit, to strengthen you and equip you for this battle. You get this strength as you pray daily, study His word daily, and stay focused on Him. When you do this, your Ephesians 6 armor is on and you are prepared for battle! When you are walking daily like this, you are able to exercise self-control and not let your anger get triggered.

Galatians 5:25 is a key summary verse. If we are walking by the Spirit, it means we seek Him daily through prayer and Bible study and that our focus is going to be on Him and not on our self. When a situation arises, try just stopping for a moment, thinking through the situation with a clear head, and praying for His wisdom. Our reactions to circumstances should be based on Godly principles (as learned from studying His word) and not based on out of control emotions such as anger.

Take a few minutes and go back and read each of the verses in Chapter 1. These are your weapons in the fight against anger! The word of God is powerful and is to be used as part of your armor (read Ephesians 6:10-18). So memorizing verses and knowing where to find verses in your Bible is a valuable skill to develop not only to manage your anger but for daily living in general!

Now let's take a look at the three Angry Situations you described in the previous chapter. Remembering the verses from Chapter 1 and the fruit of the spirit information that you just reviewed here, take a look at your reactions in each situation and think how you could have reacted differently. Write down what would have been a better way to manage that situation.

Angry Situation #1

My reaction: _____

_____

_____

_____

_____

_____

A better reaction: _____

_____

_____

_____

_____

_____

Angry Situation #2

My reaction: _____

_____

_____

_____

_____

_____

A better reaction: _____

_____

_____

_____

_____

_____

Angry Situation #3

My reaction: _____

_____

_____

_____

_____

_____

A better reaction: _____

_____

_____

_____

_____

_____

_____

Angry Situations in General

Based on all that you've read so far, what do you think would be some good things to do when you recognize you are getting angry?

1. _____

_____

_____

2. _____

_____

_____

3. _____

_____

_____

4. _____

_____

_____

Week 4 – Conflict resolution

Conflict, when not managed properly, can trigger anger and cause all sorts of problems. The goal of this chapter is to take a look at some strategies that you can use to manage conflict and keep away from those 'anger triggers'. It is important to recognize that God sometimes uses conflict to bring issues to light and encourage confession and repentance. Conflict can be between you and a friend, between you and a stranger, or between two other people.

Being able to discern when to talk and when to be silent is important and getting God's input on how to respond is also important. There are Bible verses that support both the active and involved course of action as well as the quiet and 'take it' course of action.

Iron sharpens iron, and one man sharpens another
-Proverbs 27:17

Proverbs 27:17 talks about iron sharpening iron. That means actively and boldly, yet compassionately, interacting with your friends, challenging them, confronting sin with them, encouraging them, and praying with them.

The vexation of a fool is known at once, but the
prudent ignores an insult.
-Proverbs 12:16

On the other hand, Proverbs 12:16 talks about a fool reacting to a situation (probably like a thoughtless or 'knee jerk' type of reaction) versus a prudent or smart man who overlooks an insult (or something that normally would be an anger trigger for you).

So how do you decide which is the right course of action for you to take? To confront or to be silent? You should ask yourself a few questions to help you decide what the best response is.

1. Why do I believe I need to personally get involved? Do I have some responsibility for what is happening?

2. Is there someone else who would be better equipped or has more of a responsibility to get involved?

3. How important is this situation to God?

You should also pray and ask for God's wisdom and then heed His instructions. Jesus provided a great example of how to approach conflict in Matthew 7:3-5 (it is listed in Chapter 1).

Sometimes, taking a deep breath before leaping into a situation is the smart thing to do. As Jesus points out, you first need to take the plank out of your own eye so you can see the situation clearly and from His perspective. We can think we know best or we have the best answer because of our past experiences when in reality, God has a different response in mind. That's why Jesus says to first remove the plank from your eye (your biased immediate reactions), and let Him lead you in what you should do.

Post-quiz

What is anger?

What makes me angry?

What do I do when I get angry?

What will I do differently when I get angry?

What are the 3 Bible verses you picked from Chapter 1 to remember about anger? Can you write them from memory on the next page? If you want to, you can tear out the next page and put it in your pocket and as you walk around the rec yard, read it and work on memorizing them!

Memory Verse 1:

_____

_____

_____

_____

Memory Verse 2:

_____

_____

_____

_____

Memory Verse 3:

_____

_____

_____

_____

Summary

You have taken a look at anger: what it is, what the Bible says about it, what triggers it, what reactions you have to it, and how to manage it. Hopefully you now have a better understanding and a better ability to manage your anger and to deal with others when they are angry.

You can review this book anytime you feel angry or are dealing with the anger of others.

If you just read this book on your own, you may want to share it with your Christian leadership team and see if you can organize a Bible study/class focused on anger management!

Appendix 1 – Being angry at God

This is an extra section of study that reviews the topic of being angry at God.

Have you ever gotten angry at God when you, or someone you love, go through hard times? If so, you aren't alone. In fact, many people get angry with God from time to time.

People who get mad at God often feel guilty about their anger, thinking it makes God angry with them. Their guilt sometimes drives them into feeling condemned, or distant from God.

So how should you respond when you are angry at God?

Start with prayer and ask Him to help you understand and to speak to you as you read Psalm 13:1-11 and Psalm 22:1-6. In these verses, David is pretty honest about his feelings and is letting God know! After you read these verses, answer the questions on the following pages.

Psalm 13:1-11:

How long, O Lord? Will you forget me forever? How long will you hide your face from me? How long must I take counsel in my soul and have sorrow in my heart all the day? How long shall my enemy be exalted over me? Consider and answer me, O Lord my God; light up my eyes, lest I sleep the sleep of death, lest my enemy say, "I have prevailed over him," lest my foes rejoice because I am shaken. But I have trusted in your steadfast love; my heart shall rejoice in your salvation. I will sing to the Lord, because he has dealt bountifully with me. All who see me mock me; they make mouths at me; they wag their heads. He trusts in the Lord; let him deliver him; let him rescue him, for he delights in him!" Yet you are he who took me from the womb; you made me trust you at my mother's breasts. On you was I cast from my birth, and from my mother's womb you have been my God. Be not far from me, for trouble is near, and there is none to help.

Psalm 22:1-6:

My God, my God, why have you forsaken me? Why are you so far from saving me, from the words of my groaning? O my God, I cry by day, but you do not answer, and by night, but I find no rest. Yet you are holy, enthroned on the praises of Israel. In you our fathers trusted; they trusted, and you delivered them. To you they cried and were rescued; in you they trusted and were not put to shame. But I am a worm and not a man, scorned by mankind and despised by the people.

What part of these Psalms spoke to you the most? Why?

_____

_____

_____

_____

_____

_____

What do you think about David complaining so openly to God?

_____

_____

_____

_____

_____

_____

How did David conclude his complaint? Why do you think he ended it this way?

_____

_____

_____

_____

_____

_____

What did you learn about being angry at God?

_____

_____

_____

_____

_____

_____

Appendix 2 – The four types of love in the Bible

Agape is selfless, sacrificial, unconditional love, the highest of the four types of love in the Bible. An example is found in John 14:21

> *Whoever has my commandments and keeps them, he it is who loves me. And he who loves me will be loved by my Father, and I will love him and manifest myself to him.*

Eros is the physical, sensual love such as between a husband and wife. Read the Song of Solomon in the Old Testament to get the idea of this type of love.

Philia means close friendship or brotherly love in Greek. An example is found in Romans 12:10:

> *Love one another with brotherly affection. Outdo one another in showing honor.*

Storge is family love, the bond among mothers, fathers, sisters and brothers. Examples of this type of love are seen in Jacob's love for his sons, in the love Mary and Martha had for their brother Lazarus, and even in the fifth of the Ten Commandments found in Exodus 20:12:

> *Honor your father and your mother, that your days may be long in the land that the Lord your God is giving you.*

Completion Certificate

Anger Management completion certificates are available on request. Have your institution's Chaplain send an email to 12wcert@gmail.com requesting the certificate and providing the spelling of your name as you would like it to appear on the certificate. Your Chaplain will receive a PDF file back within a week that can be printed out and presented to you. Make sure you get a copy of the completion certificate to your Case Manager so it can be in your file and available for classification review, Parole Board review, etc.

KEITH ROYS

Additional Resources

Listed below are other resources for inmates, their friends and family, and for prison ministry teams. Additional information is available at www.solidrock724.com.

12 Week Bible Study for Inmates
This is a 12 week Bible study specifically written for inmates. It asks you to commit to spending about 20 minutes a day, every day, for the next 12 weeks. Each week has a key theme and that week's verses examine the theme in depth. The themes are designed to help you rebuild your foundation in the word of God during your incarceration. A completion certificate is available.

The 90 Day Challenge, Vol 1 & Vol 2
Two books, each with 90 days of devotionals for inmates to read and reflect on with thought provoking questions and space to record reflections, prayer requests, and praises. They are designed to help an inmate grow in faith, obedience, and trust in the Lord.

The ABC's of Surviving Prison as a Christian
This provides a basic overview of what to expect and actions to take before, during, and after prison.

Bible Games and Activities for Inmates
These games and activities are designed to provide an
alternative to the normal Bible study and to make
learning about the content of the Bible memorable and
fun! Each of these games and activities are designed for
either individual or group fun. The first few are quick and
easy and the rest can take up to an hour or longer to
complete! Instructions are provided at the beginning of
each activity. Answers are provided at the end of the
book.

Christian Leadership Training for Inmates
The information in this book is designed to be used to
train inmates serving on prison church leadership teams.
Completion certificates are available.

New Testament Survey for Inmates
This is a book by book survey of each of the 27 books of
the New Testament of the Bible. An overview of each
book is provided followed by an outline, a verse or two to
memorize, and then some questions for you to answer.
The questions start easy and then get more challenging.
Some are fill in the blank type questions. Others ask you
to read some verses and then apply them to your life
right now as you sit in prison. A completion certificate is
available.

Solid Rock Ministries Inmate Order Form

Go to www.solidrock724.com for book descriptions. All books will be shipped from Amazon's Createspace publishing company. Send this order form along with a check or money order made out to Solid Rock Ministries to: Solid Rock Ministries, PO Box 38497, Baltimore, MD 21231. Please allow 2 to 3 weeks for shipping.

Book Title	Price	Quantity	Total
90 Day Devotionals Vol 1	$12		
90 Day Devotionals Vol 2	$12		
New Testament Survey*	$10		
Christian Leadership Training*	$15		
12 Week Bible Study*	$10		
Bible Games and Activities	$10		
ABC's of Surviving Prison	$10		
Shipping (per book)	**$2**		
		ORDER TOTAL:	

*Completion Certificate available on request

Send to:

Name:	
ID number:	
Institution:	
Street Address:	
City:	
State/Zip:	
Gift from:	

About The Author

Keith Roys lives in Maryland where he works as the Operations Manager for his friend's electrical contracting company. He is working with several other Christian men and women to establish a local mentoring program for newly released inmates who seek to grow in Christ as they reintegrate into society and renew ties with family and friends.

Over his lifetime, he has met a number of people who, like himself, have done time and have been through some significant events in their lives. Some of these men and women found God for the first time during their time of crisis while others recognized that they had strayed from Him and, as prodigals, returned to the cross. After listening to their stories and praying with them, he felt led to write some materials to encourage them and to help them grow stronger in His Word.

To God be the glory!

Made in the USA
Charleston, SC
06 December 2016